H.M. ADAMS

The Honey Hustle: A Guide to Crafting a Profitable Honey Brand

Maximizing Honey's Potential: Strategies for Branding, Packaging, and Marketing to Boost Profit

First edition

This book was professionally typeset on Reedsy.
Find out more at reedsy.com

To my dearest granddaughter, Mila,
In the vast tapestry of life, you are the sparkling thread that adds sweetness to every moment. Your laughter is a melody that fills my heart with joy, and your presence brings a warmth that brightens even the darkest of days.
With All My Love,
Grandma

Contents

1 Introduction   1

2 Honey's Rich History   4

3 The Science of Honey   14

4 Honey Varietals   19

5 The Versatility of Honey   22

6 DIY Honey Flavors and Recipes   27

7 Not the Fun Part - Rules and Regulations   47

8 Branding and Packaging   53

9 Selling Your Honey Products   60

10 Online Sales & Social Media   70

11 Advertising & Networking Tips   79

12 Conclusion - The Sweet Road to Success   86

13 References   88

1

Introduction

On a whim, I made a detour from the slow-moving traffic of a Southern California freeway. It was one of those days when the traffic felt particularly suffocating. I took an exit on my way home from work and decided to take a chance on the back roads. At a small intersection, I noticed a guy selling honey on a corner. I quickly glanced at the few tables as I slowly drove by, it became evident that the only thing the "stand guy" had in abundance was jars upon jars of honey – a commodity already taking up space in my pantry.

So, I pressed on, winding through the back roads, my mind wandering into contemplation. What homemade creations could the "stand guy" have made with all that surplus of honey, to attract more customers... and sales.

And then, as I crept slowly on, I encountered yet another honey stand. It seemed that honey flowed as freely as the ceaseless traffic in these parts. The one redeeming quality of Southern California's hideous traffic jams (even on the back roads) is the luxury of time for thought during the drive home.

This book was born from my attempt to serve the unknown "stand guy." It's a big shout-out to them, hoping they will produce a variety of honey products, and become more profitable. Imagine the next weary driver, seeking an escape from the freeway chaos, finding more than just jars of honey – a quick break from the slow moving traffic and a good reason to stop and leave the car.

For those contemplating the world of honey products, this book extends a helping hand.

I've looked back at honey to understand what a truly unique gift from nature we have on our hands.

So, allow me to share some tidbits of honey's history with you – a substance that has been part of human history since the beginning. This tasty gift held profound cultural significance in that it captured the attention of poets, scholars, and anyone with an appreciation for the finer things in life.

Consider this book your time-traveling companion, a condensed journey back to the origins of honey, where ancient traditions and rituals elevated it to a status of reverence.

But we won't be confined to the past. Together, we'll explore why honey remains relevant today – from its enduring role in natural remedies to becoming an indispensable ingredient in skincare and cooking.

By understanding the history of honey, you may find a better path or idea of how you wish to market or convey your brand.

I've included tips on how to package, brand, and market your honey products and have added tips on how to attract customers to your honey brand.

So let's go!

2

Honey's Rich History

oney, the luscious golden nectar, extends beyond its lip-smacking sweet goodness. It's got a history that's as rich and fascinating as syrup itself. This chapter quickly examines honey's ancient beginnings, mythological stories, and cultural significance. You're in for a treat as we unravel the layers of fascination with this liquid gold.

If you are looking for branding ideas for your honey, this mini look back in time might inspire you.

Honey's First Appearance

Let's turn back the clock to the days of prehistoric times and cave dwellers. Bees, those original architects of the golden elixir, have been doing their bee-dancing thing for a staggering 100 million years – they're practically the seasoned pros of Earth. Now, picture our ancient relatives, the hunter-gatherers, roaming the lands more than 10,000 years ago. Stumbling upon hidden honeycombs in the wild must've been like stumbling upon nature's candy aisle! A wonderful surprise that sparked a deep connection with the wild world.

Honey wasn't only a sweet treat for these ancient souls; it was a game-changer, a survival tool when times got tough. Why? Because honey had this incredible power – it could last a long time without going bad. It was a valuable resource that could be stored away for harsh winters or when the food supply ran dry. And they didn't mind enduring a few bee stings in pursuing this golden treasure. Ouch!

Fast forward to our ancestors transitioning from nomads to settled farmers, when the light bulb moment hit – beekeeping. Taming bees and taking the reins of honey production became the secret to a more dependable stash of liquid gold. The proof is etched in rock art in Algeria and Spain, depicting humans, thousands of years ago, extracting honey from beehives.

Honey's Legends and Tales

Let's take a journey through the world of honey, where its significance goes beyond a culinary delight; it's a cultural and mythological sensation. Picture ancient Greece, where honey takes center stage in mythology. Meet the Melissae, nymphs devoted to beekeeping and revered as priestesses of Demeter, the goddess of harvest. Their dance with honey symbolizes the perfect collaboration between nature and humans working together.

This tale is a captivating story of Demeter and Persephone, shedding light on why honey held such a special place in ancient Greek culture.

****

Demeter, the goddess of harvest, had a daughter named Persephone, known for her beauty. One day, as Persephone frolicked in a meadow, she was struck by the sight of a beautiful flower. As she reached down to pluck it, the ground suddenly split open, and Hades, the underworld god, emerged. He swiftly abducts Persephone and takes her to the dark world.

Demeter was heartbroken and furious. She searched for her daughter. In her grief, she neglected her duties, causing crops to wither and the earth to turn barren. Zeus, the king of the gods, intervened and demanded Hades release Persephone.

However, Persephone had tasted a pomegranate in the underworld, tying her to that world. A compromise was struck, allowing Persephone to spend part of the year with Hades and the rest with her mother.

When Persephone returned, Demeter's happiness revived the earth for spring and summer. But when Persephone returned to the underworld, Demeter grieved, and the earth fell into the cold of autumn and winter.

In Greek mythology, the story of Demeter and Persephone explains the changing seasons, showing the everlasting cycle of life, death, and rebirth.

****

Now, let's explore Norse mythology, where honey is crucial in the fascinating tale of the Mead of Poetry.

Mead is an alcoholic beverage made by fermenting honey with water. It can also include various fruits, spices, grains, or hops for flavor. Mead is one of the oldest known alcoholic drinks, with a rich history dating back thousands of years. The taste of mead can range from sweet to dry, and it may be still, carbonated, or naturally sparkling. It has cultural significance in various societies and is often associated with mythology and historical traditions.

This magical mead's origin involves Kvasir, a wise being created from the combined saliva of Aesir and Vanir gods. Unfortunately, Kvasir meets a tragic end at the hands of two dwarves.

These dwarves, seeking to gain their powers, slyly invited Kvasir to their home, where they betrayed and killed him, draining his blood. To make matters worse, the dwarves mixed Kvasir's blood with honey, creating a magical elixir known as the Mead of Poetry. This special mead could make people more creative and wise when they drink it.

So, even though Kvasir had a sad ending, his spirit continued in the magical mead, making a significant mark on Norse mythology.

****

In ancient Egypt, honey was considered a powerful remedy. The Ebers Papyrus, a medical text from around 1550 BCE, tells us how much Egyptians valued honey for its healing properties. They used it for various things, like treating wounds and even preserving the bodies of their pharaohs.

The Ebers Papyrus is like an ancient recipe book where honey is the star ingredient. Egyptians, who were pretty smart about medicine, relied on honey for its sweet taste and ability to help heal the body.

Honey was the go-to medicine for different health issues. They used it to care for wounds because it had natural properties that fought bacteria and reduced swelling. It was also like a magic potion that could make people feel better.

Honey wasn't only for healing. It also played a significant role in important ceremonies in ancient Egypt. When it came to burying their pharaohs, Egyptians believed in preserving their bodies for the afterlife. Honey was part of the unique process they used to mummify the bodies. Its natural ability to preserve things helped keep the pharaohs' bodies in good condition for their journey into the afterlife.

From the ancient Ebers Papyrus, we learn that honey in Egypt symbolized health, healing, and a close connection between nature and people. The Egyptians highly valued honey.

Honey's Cultural Significance

Now, let's explore the cultural significance of honey. In the Jewish tradition of Rosh Hashanah, honey isn't just for taste; it's an expression of hope, a wish for a year filled with blessings and sweetness—a symbolic start to something new.

Honey is part of wedding ceremonies in many cultures, each with significance and symbolism.

In some Greek weddings, a silver spoonful of honey is consumed by the couple at the end of the ceremony to symbolize happiness. Honey symbolizes the sweetness of married life.

Persian couples may participate in a Honey Kiss, where the bride and groom dip their fingers in honey and feed it to each other right before the groom kisses the bride.

Within Jewish tradition, weddings associate honey with the sweetness of life. It is often incorporated into rituals, such as the Seven Blessings recited during the ceremony, where one blessing expresses the wish for the couple to experience the sweetness of life together.

In Hindu weddings, honey is used in various rituals, symbolizing purity and sweetness. The couple may share spoonfuls of honey to ensure a sweet and harmonious union.

In some Middle Eastern cultures, honey is common in wedding celebrations. It may be included in the wedding feast or exchanged between the bride and groom to symbolize a sweet and prosperous life.

In Ethiopian weddings, honey wine (similar to Mead), known as "Tej," is often shared during the ceremony. It symbolizes the sweetness of the union and the hope for a joyous and prosperous life together.

In these cultures, honey is chosen for its sweetness and positive qualities like harmony and prosperity. It's added to wedding ceremonies to bless the newlyweds and symbolize wishes for a joyful and fulfilling marriage.

In China, honey symbolizes prosperity and good fortune, with the word "fengmi" literally incorporating the character for "bee." It's a nod to diligence and hard work.

The Bible references honey in Christianity, symbolizing God's abundant blessings in the promised land flowing with "milk and honey." This special golden liquid reminds us of the ancient Hebrews, who used it to sweeten their religious offerings.

Honey is a living piece of history, a character in myths, and a symbol that transcends cultures. Pretty sweet, huh? See what I did there?

Honey in Ancient Rituals

The Ancient Greeks took the honey celebration to a whole new level. In their mythology, honey wasn't just a sugary snack; it was the feast of the gods on Mount Olympus. Imagine honey as this sacred pipeline to immortality, often linked with ambrosia, the godly grub. It was like sipping from the fountain of divine wisdom for those savvy enough to take a dip.

In ancient Rome, honey was often used in religious rituals as an offering to the gods. It symbolized sweetness, purity, and divine blessings. Romans included honey in sacrifices and unique desserts, believing it would please the gods and bring prosperity.

As our human journey marched on, so did our methods of honey production. Beekeepers, the first honey handlers, started raising bees and making beehives to gather honey more easily. In ancient China, Egypt, and Greece, they kept bees in different vessels like clay pots and straw hives. It was the transition from wild bee roulette to the more controlled beekeeping we see thriving today.

Honey in Art and Literature

Honey has been a muse for writers and artists throughout history. You can say it has added a touch of sweetness to their creativity. Rumi, the 13th-century poet, wrote, *"This is what love does and continues to do. It tastes like honey to adults and milk to children."* The Book of Love: Poems of Ecstasy and Longing.

Artists, too, have been drawn to honey. In the painting *"The Discovery of Honey by Bacchus"* by Italian artist Piero di Cosimo, we see the mythical moment when Bacchus discovers honey.

From the storytellers of old to contemporary modern visionaries, honey keeps infusing various flavors into the artistic landscape.

Who would have thought this golden, sticky condiment we spread on our toast had such a rich and vital history?

We've dabbled enough in the past. Let's move on to modern-day times.

Modern-Day Uses of Honey

In the hustle of today's world, honey still holds its cultural importance.

Let's explore the essence of Thanksgiving in the good ol' U.S.A. The main attraction? It's not the turkey in many households, but the honey-glazed ham, claiming its place at the center of the dinner table. Beyond being a dish, it embodies the warmth and sweetness of family get-togethers and coziness. The honey glaze isn't just a culinary delight; it's a pot of holiday togetherness crafted with love and care.

But honey's not confined to the kitchen these days. It's wearing different hats, making its mark in beauty products and alternative medicine. With its antibacterial and antioxidant superpowers, honey has become a go-to in skincare and various home remedies. People are jumping on the bandwagon, incorporating this golden elixir into their lives to boost health and radiance.

Today, there are many uses for honey. Here are just a few:

- The sweetener in beverages.
- A nutritional supplement.
- A skincare ingredient.
- A culinary ingredient in salads, dressings, and marinades.
- A natural remedy for coughs and sore throats.
- Energy boost for athletes and fitness enthusiasts.
- A hair care ingredient in masks and treatments.
- Flavor enhancer for yogurt, cheese, and fruits.
- A drizzle over pancakes, waffles, and charcuterie boards.
- A natural preservative in certain food products.
- A baking ingredient in cakes, cookies, and bread.
- It is used in weight loss routines.
- Facial cleanser in skincare routines.
- Packaged as gifts or party favors.
- It is used in honey infusions with herbs, spices, or fruits.

In a nutshell, honey is more than a sweet treat for your taste buds; it carries a cultural legacy. From its role in ancient religious ceremonies to inspiring artists and writers, honey's story continues in contemporary celebrations and wellness practices. It stands as the original gift from nature, linking us to our roots and promising a sweet future.

After this little tour through the honey wonderland, you might think, "Now, how can I turn this golden goodness into some sweet profit?" Well, my friend, the hive's the limit! (Ha! Sorry, that was bad).

Let's shift our focus to the honey itself. Once we uncover how honey is created and explore its wide range of varieties, you'll gain the knowledge needed to develop top-tier and truly delightful products infused with high-quality honey.

3

The Science of Honey

lright, let's take a stroll into the fascinating world of honey. In this chapter, we'll dive into the intricate process of honey-making. Imagine these little bees diligently transforming nectar into honey, and consider how environmental factors subtly influence the flavor. It's an educational journey, shedding light on the delicate dance between nature's elements and the creation of a culinary wonder.

The Incredible Process of Honey Production

Enter the world of honey production, a fascinating process orchestrated by our little buzzing friends, the bees. Picture diligent workers in the insect realm collecting nectar from flowers, the crucial raw material for honey.

As these hardworking bees flit from one flower to the next, their specialized tool, *the proboscis*, which resembles a long, hairy tongue, acts like a straw extracting the nectar—a sweet liquid flowers create to entice pollinators.

Now, let the enchantment unfold. Well, enchantment to some, maybe a little gross to others.

The collected nectar initially stops in the bees' unique stomach, where enzymes initiate the magical process. Complex sugars begin their transformation into simpler forms like glucose and fructose. But hold on, we're just scratching the surface.

Back at the hive, bees work together like a well-coordinated team. Like skilled chefs, they share partially processed nectar by regurgitating it into the mouths of their fellow workers. These dedicated bees carry on the digestion process, breaking down sugars further.

Through a series of regurgitation and digestion cycles, the initially thin nectar undergoes a magical metamorphosis. Gradually and indeed, it thickens and evolves into the liquid gold we identify as honey. It is genuinely a fantastic collaboration and teamwork that creates this gift from nature.

If you get the chance, check out the numerous videos available online showcasing the fascinating process of how bees create honey.

The Magical Nectar-Making Bees

The heart of honey production lies in the magical bees themselves. A single honeybee can visit hundreds of flowers in a single trip, collecting nectar and pollinating along the way, thus supporting plant reproduction. Bees and plants have a special connection that keeps ecosystems going and gives us honey, this wonderful and precious gift from nature.

Worker bees, all female, perform most of the tasks within the hive, from collecting nectar to defending the hive, caring for the queen, and even producing beeswax. Turning nectar into honey highlights the amazing coordination and teamwork essential to the honey-making process.

The making of honey is a mesmerizing journey, from the incredible process of nectar collection to the magical abilities of honeybees. This chapter has only scratched the surface of this enchanting world. I reiterate that honey is not just a sweet substance in a jar; it's a product of nature's intricate balance and the diligent work of countless tiny, winged artisans.

The Medicinal Properties of Honey

In natural remedies, honey is like a golden magic potion with a history as fascinating as its golden color. It's more than a saccharine; honey has been valued for its healing powers for centuries.

Honey, often called liquid gold, is a champion for health. It's got this incredible power to fight off bacteria and infections because of the hydrogen peroxide produced in honey. This natural antibiotic ability makes honey helpful in treating cuts and wounds, stopping infections, and helping things heal faster.

Honey is also great at calming inflammation. It has antioxidants that can help soothe irritated tissues, making it excellent for sore throats and coughs, and it can thin mucous. Plus, it's thick, creating a protective layer that relieves irritated parts inside your body.

A warm cup of honey-infused tea before bedtime is often recommended for those battling insomnia. Honey's natural sugars raise insulin levels slightly, promoting the release of serotonin, the mood-regulating hormone, contributing to a sense of relaxation and, in turn, aiding in a more restful night's sleep.

Warning! - Demystifying Honey Myths

Despite the admiration for honey's health benefits, it is important to dispel a few myths. One common misconception suggests that all honey is created equal. The truth is the type and quality of honey can significantly impact its therapeutic attributes. Raw, unprocessed honey retains a wealth of beneficial compounds compared to the heavily processed varieties on many supermarket shelves.

Another myth often heard is that honey is a cure-all for every ailment. While honey does offer numerous health benefits, it cannot substitute professional medical advice or treatments for serious conditions. It plays a complementary role, most effectively partnered with conventional medical approaches.

Giving honey to infants or children below the age of 1 year is NOT recommended. This precaution is due to the potential presence of a bacterium known as Clostridium in honey, which could lead to infant botulism.

4

Honey Varietals

Bees are vital for making honey, but the environment around them also affects how the honey looks and tastes.

Floral Varieties and Flavors

The honey's flavor, color, and smell can change significantly depending on the flowers the bees get nectar from. That's because each type of flower gives the honey its unique taste. For example, honey from clover flowers is light and not too strong, but if bees gather nectar from wildflowers, the honey can have a more mixed and exciting flavor. Other things like the dirt, the weather, and the time of year can also make the honey turn out different.

Where the hive is and what plants are nearby also have a say in how the final honey turns out.

The world of honey is like a buffet of flavors, each with its unique taste.

Let's look at the top 12 honey flavors and their origins:

- *Clover Honey:* Light and simple, this honey comes from the nectar of clover flowers. It's a classic choice, milder than most honey and sweet.
- *Wildflower Honey:* Picture bees buzzing around various wildflowers. That's the source of this honey's diverse and rich flavor, like nature's blend.
- *Orange Blossom Honey:* Bees collect nectar from flowers in orange groves, producing honey with a citrusy zest and a delicate floral essence.
- *Lavender Honey:* If you've ever been to a lavender field, you'll get why this honey is so special. It has a fragrant, soothing flavor, almost like a stroll through the purple fields.
- *Buckwheat Honey:* This honey is dark, bold, and robust. Buckwheat flowers give it a strong, almost molasses-like taste.
- *Acacia Honey:* Gentle and velvety, this honey originates from the nectar of acacia flowers. It's often a top pick for its light and almost fruity flavor.
- *Manuka Honey:* Hailing from New Zealand, Manuka Honey is like the rock star of the honey world. It's known for its strong taste and potential health benefits. It's also much more expensive than most honey.
- *Eucalyptus Honey:* Eucalyptus trees are a favorite among bees, and the honey derived from their flowers carries a menthol-like kick, making it stand out with a fresh flavor.
- *Blueberry Honey:* As it sounds, this honey comes from bees busy among blueberry blossoms. It captures a bit of that fruity goodness.
- *Sage Honey:* Found in the Western United States, sage honey has a unique herbal flavor. It has a wild taste with a touch of earthiness.
- *Thyme Honey:* Bees collecting nectar from thyme plants craft this

honey with a savory, herby twist. It's a culinary pleasure.

- *Fireweed Honey:* Fireweed Honey is sometimes called the "Champagne of Honey." It's smooth and clear, matching its light but fancy flavor. Bees make this honey by gathering nectar from the pink flowers of fireweed plants in North America. The name "fireweed" comes from the dormant seeds in the soil that are left for long periods until a wildfire comes along. After the fire, the seeds wake up, and beautiful flowers bloom.

Each of these honey flavors is like a little tasty work of art made by nature and the hardworking bees that gather nectar from all sorts of flowers across the globe. There are many other varieties to experience; these are just a few.

So, the next time you dip your spoon into a jar of honey, remember you're enjoying the essence of the flowers and the landscapes they originate from.

5

The Versatility of Honey

B y now, it's clear that Honey goes beyond a drizzle for our pancakes. This chapter will explore the many ways we use honey today.

The Art of Honey Tasting

Tasting honey is like diving into the fancy world of wine or coffee, where you need a skilled taste bud. People who taste honey pay attention to the sweetness, tanginess, and how it feels in their mouth. The texture can be anywhere from drippy to creamy, and sometimes, the aftertaste sticks around with hints of herbs or spices. It's like a whole art form.

Think of it like a wine expert – they can pick up all the fancy details in a glass of wine. Well, a Honey sommelier does the same thing. They appreciate the skill that goes into making each jar of honey.

And just like how wine shows off where its grapes come from, honey carries the vibe of the place it's made. Acacia honey from the cool valleys of Hungary has this light and almost see-through sweetness. In contrast, Manuka honey from the far-off lands of New Zealand has this deep, earthy flavor with some bonus therapeutic stuff going on. The weather, soil, and all the different flowers hanging around give each kind of honey its unique personality. It's like a taste adventure from different corners of the world.

Why Some Types of Honey Are More Expensive

Its sweetness does not solely determine the price of honey but is influenced by factors such as rarity, production methods, and labor intensity. Manuka honey, renowned for its medicinal properties, commands a premium due to the meticulous care required in harvesting and the limited flowering window of the Manuka tree. Similarly, artisanal honey from remote regions may be more expensive due to the difficulty of harvesting and the unique flavors derived from untouched landscapes.

In the rich world of honey, each jar tells a story of nature's diversity and the labor of bees and beekeepers alike. The world of honey is a journey through the fragrant fields of flowers across continents and into the refined realm of tasting mastery.

Honey-based Creations

Honey is a key player in making all sorts of tasty things, from yummy honey sauces to delicate pastries. Skilled creators use different kinds of honey to make their food extra special.

Creating honey-infused treats is like a dance, blending traditional methods with innovative ideas. Using ancient techniques, beekeepers tend their hives to produce honey with unique flavors. Subsequently, skilled chefs and artisans transform this liquid gold into an array of delights, from honey-infused chocolates to exquisite spreads. The key lies in comprehending honey's taste, viscosity, and crystallization process, ensuring each treat is a harmonious blend of flavors.

In the culinary world, honey serves as an artist's palette, offering endless possibilities for enthusiasts who appreciate the craftsmanship within each jar. Whether drizzling it over exquisite cheeses or incorporating it into velvety ice creams, crafting honey-infused treats is a collaboration between nature and human creativity, infusing everyday magic into our meals.

Honey as a Natural Sweetener in Cooking

Honey has been a favorite natural sweetener in cooking for a long time, offering more than just sweetness. It adds a unique depth and complexity to dishes with its floral notes. In baking, it's a healthier choice than regular sugar, bringing moisture and subtle richness to cakes, muffins, and cookies. Its natural mix of fructose and glucose releases energy slowly, making it a good option for those watching their glycemic index.

Honey is a versatile ingredient. You can use it as a glaze for meats, giving them a perfect balance of sweetness and a hint of tang. And the bonus? It has properties that support your immune system. Whether drizzling it on yogurt, blending it into salad dressings, or incorporating it into marinades, honey is a wholesome sweetener that enhances the culinary experience without compromising health.

Beauty and Wellness Products

Honey is a golden elixir known for promoting wellness and self-care. Packed with antioxidants and powerful antibacterial properties, it boosts the immune system and soothes skin conditions. Incorporating honey into your routine offers a luxurious touch, leaving the skin supple and radiant. Whether consumed internally or applied externally, honey is a versatile ally for overall wellness.

The Benefits of Honey-infused Products

Using honey-infused products unlocks numerous benefits for your skin, overall health, and hair. Honey, a natural moisture magnet, keeps your skin hydrated, giving it a radiant and smooth glow. It acts like a superhero against acne and blemishes, making it a go-to remedy for various skin issues. Beyond the surface, honey's antioxidants combat harmful elements, preventing premature aging and maintaining skin elasticity. In hair care, honey-infused products provide a treat, leaving your locks shiny and strong.

6

DIY Honey Flavors and Recipes

I n this chapter, you'll find recipes from baked goods, skincare products, and home remedies. These are only a few ideas of the many things you can create with your honey.

Throw on your creativity hat and imagine what you can create!

Exploring Creative Flavor Combinations

Honey is a versatile ingredient with a wide range of flavors. There's a world of unique honey infusions that can enhance your cooking. Explore these various and unexpected flavor pairings with honey.

Citrus Zest and Lavender Honey - The classic combination of citrus and honey becomes extraordinary with the addition of subtle floral notes from lavender. Try this blend in marinades for grilled chicken or drizzled over a summer fruit salad.

Orange Blossom Honey and Thyme - Orange blossom honey's flowery scent blends perfectly with thyme's earthy tones, making it great for glazed carrots or roasted sweet potatoes. Imagine a golden drizzle on warm cornbread.

Cinnamon Stick-Infused Honey - Steeping a cinnamon stick in honey creates a warm and comforting blend. Mix it into your morning coffee or oatmeal for a cozy start to the day. It also adds a delightful touch to baked goods like cinnamon rolls or apple pie.

Cardamom and Ginger Honey - Blend cardamom's exotic warmth with ginger's zesty kick for a honey infusion that pairs well with Asian-inspired stir-fries or as a sweetener for chai lattes. This combination adds a layer of complexity to both savory and sweet dishes.

Basil and Berry Honey - Marry the sweet essence of berries with the peppery undertones of basil for honey that pairs beautifully with summer salads, desserts, or even as a drizzle over vanilla ice cream. The herbaceous notes of basil add a surprising twist to the sweetness of the honey.

Rosemary and Lemon Honey - The woody aroma of rosemary combined with the bright zest of lemon creates a honey infusion that complements roasted vegetables, grilled chicken, or even a simple goat cheese appetizer. It's a versatile infusion that adds freshness to any dish.

Chili and Cocoa Honey - Combining honey with spicy chili and rich cocoa creates an exciting taste for those who love bold flavors. Try this spicy-sweet honey in barbecue sauces, grilled peaches, or even a hot and spicy chocolate drink.

Vanilla Bean and Cardamom Honey - Mix vanilla's luxurious scent with the warm citrus notes of cardamom to create a honey blend that turns a basic bowl of yogurt into a decadent delight. It's also an excellent addition to desserts such as panna cotta or rice pudding.

Lavender and Blueberry Honey - Mixing lavender's floral notes with the sweet taste of blueberries creates a honey blend that reminds you of a beautiful garden. Use it on pancakes, in a vinaigrette, or as a topping for lavender cheesecake. Enjoy the versatile and aromatic addition to your dishes.

Jasmine and Mint Honey - Combine the light scent of jasmine with the fresh taste of mint to create honey that goes well with green tea, summer cocktails, or a basic fruit salad. This delightful infusion adds a touch of elegance to your culinary creations.

There are countless options for creative flavor blends in the incredible world of honey. These examples are just a few - don't hesitate to try new combinations and find your unique honey mix. Follow your taste buds, savoring honey's diverse symphony of flavors.

Creating and selling honey-made products involves adherence to various rules and regulations to ensure product safety, quality, and compliance with relevant standards. The specific rules can vary by country and region, so it's essential to check with local authorities and regulatory bodies.

Disclaimer: The following pages are suggestions and DIY-type recipes not approved for commercial sale. Please check with your local health departments or food agencies if you wish to create products for sale.

Culinary Delights - Baking with Honey

Honey-Lemon Blueberry Muffins

Ingredients:
- 2 cups all-purpose flour
- 1/2 cup honey
- 1/2 cup unsalted butter, melted
- 1 cup fresh blueberries
- 2 large eggs
- 1 cup buttermilk
- 1 teaspoon vanilla extract
- 1 tablespoon lemon zest
- 1 teaspoon baking powder
- 1/2 teaspoon baking soda
- 1/4 teaspoon salt

Instructions:

Preheat the oven to 375°F (190°C) and line a muffin tin with paper liners. Whisk together flour, baking powder, baking soda, and salt in a bowl. Mix honey, melted butter, eggs, buttermilk, vanilla extract, and lemon zest in another bowl. Combine the wet and dry ingredients, then gently fold in the blueberries.

Divide the batter into the muffin cups and bake for 18-20 minutes or until a toothpick comes out clean.

Honey-Almond Granola Bars

Ingredients:

2 cups old-fashioned oats
1 cup almonds, chopped
1/2 cup honey
1/4 cup unsalted butter
1/4 cup brown sugar
1 teaspoon vanilla extract
1/4 teaspoon salt
1/2 cup dried fruit (e.g., raisins, cranberries)

Instructions:

Preheat the oven to 350°F (175°C) and line a baking pan with parchment paper.

Heat honey, butter, brown sugar, vanilla extract, and salt in a saucepan until melted.

In a large bowl, combine oats and chopped almonds. Pour the honey mixture over and mix well. Press the mixture into the prepared pan, and bake for 20-25 minutes or until golden brown. Allow it to cool before cutting into bars and adding dried fruit.

Honey Vanilla Bean Madeleine

Ingredients:
1 cup all-purpose flour
1/2 cup honey
2/3 cup unsalted butter, melted and cooled
3 large eggs
1 vanilla bean, seeds scraped
1/2 teaspoon baking powder
Pinch of salt
Powdered sugar (for dusting)

Instructions:

Preheat the oven to 375°F (190°C) and grease Madeleine molds. In a bowl, whisk together flour, baking powder, and salt. Beat eggs, honey, and vanilla bean seeds in another bowl until light and fluffy. Gently fold the dry ingredients, add melted butter, and mix until smooth. Spoon batter into the molds and bake for 10-12 minutes or until the edges are golden brown. Cool slightly, dust with powdered sugar (optional), and enjoy this delicate honey-infused Madeleine.

Honey Whole Wheat Bread

Ingredients:
- 2 1/4 teaspoons (1 packet) active dry yeast
- 1 1/2 cups warm water (110°F/43°C)
- 1/4 cup honey
- 3 1/2 cups whole wheat flour
- 1/4 cup unsalted butter, melted
- 1 1/2 teaspoons salt
- 1 tablespoon olive oil (for greasing)

Instructions:

Activate the Yeast:

In a small bowl, combine warm water and honey. Stir until the honey dissolves.

Sprinkle the yeast over the water and let it sit for about 5 minutes until it becomes frothy.

Prepare the Dough:

In a large mixing bowl, combine the whole wheat flour and salt. Create a well in the center and pour in the activated yeast mixture and melted butter. Mix until a dough forms.

Knead the Dough:
Transfer the dough to a floured surface and knead for about 8-10 minutes until it becomes smooth and elastic.
Place the dough in a greased bowl, cover it with a damp cloth, and let it rise in a warm place for 1-2 hours or until it doubles in size.

Shape the Loaf:
Punch down the risen dough and transfer it to a floured surface. Shape the dough into a rectangle, then roll it tightly to form a loaf.

Second Rise:
Place the shaped dough into a greased loaf pan. Cover with a damp cloth and let it rise for another 30-45 minutes.

Preheat and Bake:
Preheat the oven to 375°F (190°C) during the second rise. Brush the top of the loaf with a bit of honey for a glossy finish. Bake for 25-30 minutes or until the bread is golden brown and sounds hollow when tapped on the bottom.

Cool and Enjoy:
Allow the bread to cool in the pan for 10 minutes, then transfer it to a wire rack to cool completely before slicing.

This honey whole wheat bread is perfect for sandwiches or enjoyed alone. The honey adds a subtle sweetness, making it a favorite for breakfast or as an accompaniment to meals. Enjoy the delightful aroma and rich flavor of freshly baked bread!

Honey-Infused Flavors

Vanilla Bean Infused Honey

Ingredients:
1 cup raw honey
1 vanilla bean, split lengthwise

Instructions:
Heat the raw honey in a small saucepan over low heat until it becomes thin and pour-able.

Add the split vanilla bean to the honey.

Allow the mixture to steep for at least 24 hours, longer for a more intense flavor. Remove the vanilla bean and transfer the honey to a glass jar. Use this fragrant vanilla-infused honey to sweeten teas and desserts or drizzle over yogurt.

Ideal Uses

- Drizzle over Greek yogurt or oatmeal.
- Add to a cup of hot black tea for a soothing vanilla twist.
- Use as a sweetener for homemade whipped cream.
- Glaze over fresh fruit like peaches or strawberries for a simple dessert.

Notes:
The subtle notes of vanilla add depth and sophistication to the honey, elevating its versatility in various culinary applications.

Cinnamon and Clove Honey

Ingredients:
  1 cup raw honey
  2 cinnamon sticks
  4-5 whole cloves

Instructions:
  In a small saucepan, warm the honey over low heat. Add cinnamon sticks and cloves to the honey. Simmer for 15-20 minutes to infuse the spices into the honey. Remove the cinnamon sticks and cloves. Allow the honey to cool before transferring it to a jar. Use this spiced honey to sweeten coffee, drizzle over pancakes, or as a glaze for roasted vegetables.

Ideal Uses

  • Swirl into a cup of chai tea or coffee for a spiced kick.
  • Drizzle over sweet potato fries or roasted butternut squash.
  • Mix with butter and spread on warm biscuits or scones.
  • Use as a glaze for baked apples or pears.

Notes:
  The warmth of cinnamon and the aromatic depth of cloves make this honey infusion perfect for adding a cozy and spiced touch to your favorite dishes.

Lemon Zest and Thyme Honey

Ingredients:

1 cup raw honey
Zest of 2 lemons
2-3 sprigs of fresh thyme

Instructions:

Combine raw honey, lemon zest, and thyme in a bowl. Allow the mixture to sit for at least 12 hours, allowing the flavors to meld. Strain out the lemon zest and thyme. Transfer the infused honey to a jar, capturing the essence of citrus and herbs. Use this honey as a glaze for grilled chicken, in salad dressings, or as a sweetener for iced tea.

Ideal Uses

- Mix into a vinaigrette for a refreshing salad dressing.
- Spread on warm toast or English muffins.
- Infuse into cocktails like a honey-thyme lemonade.
- Brush over grilled shrimp or chicken for a citrus marinade.

Notes:

The bright, citrus notes from the lemon zest and the earthy aroma of thyme create a harmonious and refreshing honey infusion.

Chili Lime Infused Honey

Ingredients:
1 cup raw honey
Zest of 2 limes
1-2 small dried red chili peppers, sliced

Instructions:

Combine raw honey, lime zest, and sliced chili peppers in a bowl. Allow the mixture to sit for at least 24 hours, allowing the flavors to meld.

Strain out the lime zest and chili peppers.

Transfer the infused honey to a jar, capturing the sweet, tangy, and spicy notes. Use this honey to add a kick to marinades, glazes for grilled meats, or drizzle over fresh fruit.

Ideal Uses

- Brush over grilled pineapple or watermelon.
- Add to a marinade for spicy lime-infused chicken skewers.
- Drizzle over avocado toast for a sweet and spicy twist.
- Mix into a dipping sauce for spring rolls or dumplings.

Notes:

The combination of zesty lime and a subtle heat from the chili peppers creates a dynamic honey infusion, perfect for those who enjoy a hint of spice in their dishes.

DIY Medicinal Honey Recipes

Important: According to Kidshealth.org, **Babies younger than 1 year old should not be given honey.** That's because a type of bacteria (called *Clostridium*) that causes infant botulism can be found in honey. Infant botulism can cause muscle weakness, with signs like poor sucking, a weak cry, constipation, and decreased muscle tone (floppiness).

Parents can help prevent infant botulism by not giving their baby honey or any processed foods that contain honey (like honey graham crackers) until after their child's first birthday. Check with your doctor before giving your baby honey.

Lollipops are not recommended for children under the age of four. You're the expert when it comes to your child. Just a gentle reminder to be cautious of any items that could pose a choking hazard to children at any age, and keep their environment safe and your child supervised while consuming a lollipop.

Honey-Elderberry Powerhouse Lollies

Ingredients:

1/4 c. Manuka Honey (Manuka is recommended, or organic raw Honey whenever possible)

1/2 c. Elderberry Syrup (Organic)

Lollipop mold (food grade)

Lollipop sticks

Candy thermometer

Instructions:

In a small saucepan on low heat, combine honey and organic elderberry syrup. Continuously stir until the honey has melted and is well combined. Increase to medium heat.

Attach the candy thermometer, ensuring it does not touch the bottom of the saucepan. Stir the mixture until temperature reaches 300°F (150°C), approximately 30 minutes.

Remove the saucepan from the heat and let it cool.

Pour mixture into the lollipop molds and quickly insert lollipop sticks. Let the lollipops harden for several hours or overnight. Once the lollipops harden, remove them from the molds and store them in an airtight container at room temperature.

Benefits of Manuka Honey

- *Antibacterial Power:* Renowned for potent antibacterial effects, thanks to MGO (Methylglyoxal is a compound found in certain types of honey, like Manuka. It's responsible for the antibacterial properties associated with Manuka honey, making it effective against a range of bacteria and microbes).
- *Sore Throat Soother:* Provides comforting relief for sore throats, especially in lollipop form.
- *Immune Boost:* Antioxidants enhance overall immune health, potentially fortifying defenses against common illnesses.
- *Digestive Support:* May positively impact digestive health and balance gut microbiota.

Benefits of Organic Elderberry

- *Antioxidant-Rich:* Packed with antioxidants protecting cells from damage.
- *Anti-Inflammatory:* Known for reducing and relieving the discomfort of inflammation.
- *Vitamin C Boost:* Naturally high in vitamin C, supporting the immune system and overall health.
- *Heart Health:* Some studies suggest positive effects, promoting good cholesterol levels and reducing heart-related risks.

Honey and Ginger Medicinal Elixir

Ingredients:
   1 cup of raw, organic honey
   1 large piece of fresh ginger (about 2 inches), peeled and grated
   1 lemon, juiced
   Optional: 1 to 2 teaspoons of turmeric powder
   Optional: A pinch of black pepper

Instructions:
   In a clean glass jar, combine the raw honey and grated ginger. Squeeze the juice of one lemon into the jar. If desired, add turmeric powder and a pinch of black pepper for additional health benefits. Both turmeric and black pepper have anti-inflammatory properties.
   Stir the mixture well until the ingredients are thoroughly combined. Seal the jar and let it sit for at least 24 hours to allow the flavors to meld and the medicinal properties to infuse into the honey.

You can consume this elixir by taking 1-2 teaspoons daily or mix it with warm water to create a soothing tea.

Note:
   Honey, ginger, lemon, turmeric, and black pepper are all known for their potential health benefits. However, it's essential to consult with a healthcare professional, especially if you have any existing health conditions or are taking medications, before incorporating new remedies into your routine.

Beauty and Skin Care

Honey & Turmeric Face Mask

Ingredients:
 1 tablespoon raw honey
 1/2 teaspoon turmeric powder
 1 teaspoon plain yogurt

Instructions:
 Mix raw honey, turmeric powder, and yogurt in a bowl until well combined. Apply the mixture to your face, avoiding the eye area. Leave the mask on for 15-20 minutes. Rinse off with warm water, gently massaging the mask into your skin. Pat your face dry and follow up with your favorite moisturizer.

Benefits:
 Honey's antibacterial properties cleanse the skin. Turmeric reduces inflammation and brightens the complexion. Yogurt soothes and moisturizes the skin.

Hydrating Honey Avocado Face Mask

Ingredients:
 1/2 ripe avocado
 2 tablespoons raw honey
 1 teaspoon plain Greek yogurt

Instructions:

Mash the avocado in a bowl.

Add raw honey and yogurt and mix until smooth. Apply the mixture to your face and neck. Leave on for 15-20 minutes. Rinse off with lukewarm water.

Benefits:

Honey moisturizes and soothes the skin.

Avocado provides nourishment and hydration.

Yogurt gently exfoliates and brightens the complexion.

Green Tea and Honey Toner

Ingredients:

1/2 cup brewed green tea, cooled

1 tablespoon raw honey

Instructions:

Combine cooled green tea with raw honey in a bowl. Submerge a cotton pad in the mixture and use it to swipe across your face as a toner after cleansing gently.

Benefits:

Honey boasts antibacterial properties, while green tea soothes and diminishes redness. Acting as a natural toner, the skin feels revitalized and refreshed.

Rosewater and Honey Brightening Serum

Ingredients:

1 tablespoon rosewater
1 teaspoon raw honey
1 tablespoon jojoba oil

Instructions:
Blend rosewater, raw honey, and jojoba oil in a small dropper bottle. Apply a few drops to your face before moisturizing, both in the morning and at night.

Benefits:
Honey adds a natural glow to the skin.
Rosewater tones and balances. Jojoba oil provides deep hydration without clogging pores.

Honey Soap

Making natural soap with honey can be a rewarding and skin-friendly project. Here's a basic recipe for honey soap.

Ingredients:
2 cups of soap base (you can use a melt-and-pour soap base or make your own soap from scratch using lye, oils, and water)
1 tablespoon of raw honey
Essential oils for fragrance (optional)
Soap molds

Instructions:
Prepare the Soap Base:
If you're using a melt-and-pour soap base, cut it into small, uniform pieces for easier melting.

If you're making soap from scratch, follow a cold or hot process soap-making method. Be sure to include oils like olive oil, coconut oil, and palm oil in your recipe.

Melt the Soap Base:

If using a melt-and-pour base, melt it according to the package instructions. This is usually done in a microwave or a double boiler.

Add Honey:

Once the soap base is melted, add 1 tablespoon of raw honey. Stir well to ensure even distribution.

Add Essential Oils (optional):

If you want to add fragrance to your soap, incorporate a few drops of your preferred essential oils. Popular choices include lavender, tea tree, or chamomile.

Pour into Molds:

Pour the melted soap mixture into your soap molds. Silicone molds are often preferred for easy removal.

Cool and Harden:

Allow the soap to cool and harden. This may take a few hours, depending on the size and depth of your molds.

Remove from Molds:

Once the soap has completely hardened, gently pop it out of the molds. If you used silicone molds, this should be an easy process.

Cure (if making from scratch):

If you made the soap from scratch, it's recommended to let it cure for a few weeks before using. This allows the soap to become milder and longer-lasting.

Enjoy:

Your honey soap is now ready to use. Enjoy the skin-nourishing benefits of honey in your handmade soap!

Remember to follow safety guidelines when working with lye or any soap-making materials. If you're new to soap making, consider starting with a melt-and-pour soap base for simplicity.

How to Extend Honey's Shelf Life

To extend the shelf life of honey, it's crucial to follow proper hygiene practices and reduce exposure to both moisture and contaminants. Always use a clean, dry spoon when scooping honey to prevent introducing foreign substances. Keep the lid tightly sealed to protect against air and humidity. Additionally, consider storing honey in the refrigerator, especially in warmer climates, to slow down crystallization. Proper storage practices ensure honey's quality for an extended period despite its long shelf life.

Rejuvenating Crystallized Honey

Crystallization is a natural process that occurs over time, causing honey to become thicker and granular. To rejuvenate crystallized honey, gently warm the jar by placing it in a bowl of warm water or using a microwave on low heat. Avoid boiling or overheating, as excessive heat can compromise honey's flavor and nutritional content. Stir the honey periodically during the warming process until the crystals dissolve, restoring it to its liquid state. This simple method revitalizes the honey's texture and allows you to savor its original smoothness and rich taste.

7

Not the Fun Part - Rules and Regulations

C reating and selling honey-made products involves adherence to various rules and regulations to ensure product safety, quality, and compliance with relevant standards. The specific rules can vary by country and region, so it's essential to check with local authorities and regulatory bodies. However, here are some general guidelines that may apply:

Food Products

Food Safety Regulations:

Ensure compliance with food safety regulations and standards set by local health departments or food agencies.

Follow good manufacturing practices (GMP) to maintain hygiene and prevent contamination.

Labeling Requirements:

Clearly and accurately label your honey-made products with information such as product name, ingredients, net weight, contact information, and any allergen warnings.

Check and adhere to specific labeling requirements for honey and related products in your region.

Honey Grading Standards:

Understand and follow any honey grading standards established by your country or region. This may include designations like Grade A, Grade B, etc.

Packaging Regulations:

Please ensure your packaging meets the relevant regulations, including food-grade materials and proper sealing to prevent contamination.

Registration and Licensing:

Register your business and obtain the necessary licenses or permits for food production and sales.

Quality Control:

Implement quality control measures to ensure the consistency and quality of your honey-made products.

Traceability:

Establish a traceability system to track your honey's origin and processing journey.

Allergen Information:

To comply with allergen labeling requirements, indicate if your product contains any common allergens, such as nuts or dairy.

Local Beekeeping Regulations:

If you're involved in beekeeping as part of your honey production, be aware of and comply with local regulations related to beekeeping, hive management, and honey extraction.

Market Regulations:

Understand and comply with any regulations related to marketing and selling honey-made products, including pricing and advertising rules.

Inspections:

Be prepared for regular inspections by relevant health or food safety authorities to ensure compliance with regulations.

Always consult with local health departments, agricultural agencies, or food safety authorities for the most accurate and up-to-date information specific to your location. Compliance with regulations not only ensures the legality of your business but also helps build trust with consumers.

Beauty Products

Creating and selling honey-based *beauty* products involves additional considerations beyond those for food products. Here are some guidelines to keep in mind:

Ingredient Safety and Cosmetic Regulations:

Verify that all ingredients in your beauty products are safe for topical use. Ensure compliance with cosmetic regulations in your region.

Follow the guidelines and restrictions set by cosmetic regulatory bodies regarding using specific ingredients.

Labeling and Packaging:

List all ingredients on the product label, following cosmetic labeling regulations.

Ensure that packaging materials are suitable for cosmetic products and provide necessary information like usage instructions, precautions, and expiration dates.

Product Claims:

Avoid making misleading or false claims about the benefits of your beauty products. Ensure that any claims are supported by scientific evidence.

Allergen Information:

Clearly label products with any potential allergens to help consumers with allergies make informed decisions.

Product Testing:

Conduct necessary safety and stability testing for your beauty products. This may include microbial, stability, and challenge testing to ensure the product's safety over time.

Good Manufacturing Practices (GMP):

Follow GMP to maintain a clean and safe manufacturing environment.

Regulatory Compliance:

Check and comply with regulations from relevant authorities overseeing cosmetics and beauty products in your country or region.

Registration and Notification:

In some jurisdictions, cosmetic products may need to be registered or notified to regulatory bodies. Check the requirements in your area.

Ethical and Sustainable Practices:

Consider incorporating ethical and sustainable practices in sourcing ingredients, production processes, and packaging, as consumer interest in these aspects is growing.

Educational Resources:

Provide educational resources for consumers, explaining the benefits of honey and other natural ingredients used in your beauty products.

Product Liability Insurance:

Consider obtaining product liability insurance to protect your business from potential legal issues arising from using your beauty products.

Remember to keep an eye on the changes in regulations, as they can evolve. Seeking legal advice or consulting with a regulatory expert in the cosmetics industry can be beneficial to ensure that your honey-based beauty products comply with all relevant laws and regulations.

8

Branding and Packaging

E mbarking on the journey of sharing your honey-inspired creations is about crafting delicious products and bringing your passion to a broader audience.

The strategies outlined here will help you establish a unique brand identity. From crafting a compelling narrative that resonates with your audience to master the particulars of packaging, this chapter is your head start for navigating the exciting opportunity of turning your honey creations into a marketable and cherished product.

Crafting a Unique Brand Identity for Your Honey Creations: Defining Your Brand's Values and Mission

Building a stand-out brand starts by digging into what matters to your brand—your values and mission. Your values are like the compass for your brand, guiding how you do business and connect with customers. Think about the core beliefs behind your honey-inspired creations. Is it about supporting sustainable beekeeping, using local ingredients, or promoting wellness through natural products? It's these values that shape your brand and make it unique.

Once you've identified your values, create a clear and concise mission statement. Your mission should reflect your brand's purpose and contribution to the world. Whether bringing the purest form of honey to consumers or fostering a community around sustainable practices, a well-defined mission sets the tone for your brand identity and provides a compass for future decisions.

Crafting a Brand Story

A compelling brand story brings together the elements of your values, mission, and journey that led to creating your honey-inspired products. It's more than a narrative; it connects your brand and audience. Begin by sharing the origin of your love for honey – whether it stems from a cherished family tradition, a captivating meeting with a local beekeeper, or a deep fascination with the wonders of nature.

Share the challenges and triumphs that shaped your journey, creating an authentic narrative that speaks directly to your target audience. Engage with the emotional aspects of your story; this connection will form a lasting impression in the minds of your customers.

Consider incorporating elements of sustainability, craftsmanship, and the inherent goodness of honey into your brand's story. Whether through your website, social media, or product packaging, consistently communicate this story to build brand loyalty.

Crafting a Consistent Tone

Consistency is vital in storytelling. Ensure that the tone of your brand story aligns with your overall brand identity. If your brand is known for its playfulness, infuse that playfulness into your narrative. If it's about trust and reliability, let those qualities shine through. A consistent tone helps customers form a clear and lasting impression of your brand.

Designing a Memorable Logo and Packaging

Creating a memorable logo is essential for your honey brand. Think about using warm, golden colors and simple designs like a beehive or flying bee to tell your brand story. Hire a graphic designer to create a flexible logo. Packaging is also essential; ensure it reflects your brand values, uses Eco-friendly materials, and ensures functionality.

When designing, packaging, labeling, and considering sustainability for your honey products, consider the following key factors.

Packaging and Labeling Your Honey Creations

Attractive Packaging

The exterior is the first interaction consumers have with your brand. Its design plays a significant role in capturing the attention of potential customers. A well-designed package conveys the essence of your honey creations.

Aesthetics and Branding

Opt for warm and natural color palettes when designing products inspired by honey. Consider the strategic placement of your logo, ensuring it is prominent and easy to remember. A well-crafted logo represents your brand identity, so please invest your time creating a design that resonates with your audience.

Functionality and Protection

While aesthetics are important, functionality is equally crucial. Honey is sensitive to environmental factors like light and moisture, which can affect its quality. Choose packaging that provides a protective barrier against these elements. For instance, jars with tight-sealing lids maintain the honey's freshness and integrity.

Size and Portability

Consider convenience. Squeeze bottles or travel-sized jars for on-the-go, sturdy packaging for larger quantities.

Labeling Regulations and Guidelines

Labeling is not only about making your product look good; it's also a legal and ethical responsibility. Understanding and following labeling regulations ensures transparency with your customers and avoids potential legal issues.

Educate Through Labels

Use your labels to educate consumers about the sustainability initiatives you've embraced. If your packaging is made from recycled materials, highlight this on the label. If you support bee-friendly practices, share this information with your customers.

Nutritional Information

Include a comprehensive list of nutritional information on your label, adhering to the guidelines set by regulatory bodies. Highlight the critical dietary components of your honey, such as calories, sugars, and any additional ingredients.

Ingredient List

List all the ingredients used in your honey creations. If your honey is infused with additional flavors or contains allergens, ensure this information is prominent. This transparency builds trust with consumers.

Allergen Warnings

If your honey product includes common allergens like nuts, soy, or dairy, it's imperative to include allergy warnings. This helps allergy-conscious customers make informed choices and is legally required in many regions.

Country of Origin

Indicate where your honey comes from. This is important for people who enjoy honey from specific places or want to support local products. Plus, it follows labeling rules in many countries.

Batch Numbers and Expiry Dates

Assign a batch number to each production run, including the manufacturing or packaging date. Clearly state the expiry date so customers know the product's freshness. This information is crucial for meeting regulatory requirements and instilling confidence in consumers.

Choosing Sustainable Packaging Options

Materials

Opt for recyclable, biodegradable, or renewable resource-based packaging. Glass jars and paper-based packaging are good options.

Minimalist Design

Consider a minimalist design to reduce excessive packaging.

Reusable Packaging

Explore options for reusable packaging. If your packaging (i.e., a jar) is reusable and your label is excellent, it may also remind the customer to replenish their product whenever they reuse it—another potential sale.

Local Sourcing

Opt for packaging materials sourced locally whenever possible to support local businesses and reduce the carbon footprint associated with transportation.

Packaging and labeling tell a story about your honey. In an Eco-conscious world, sustainable choices aren't just popular but a responsibility. Connect with consumers through a story that aligns with their values, making Eco-friendly packaging a will and a necessity.

So, when working on how your honey looks and what goes on the label, remember that each part is a chance to show off what makes your honey unique. With good design, clear labels, and Eco-friendly choices, your honey can positively impact the planet and the people who love it.

Don't rush it. Invest time in creating a consistent and cohesive visual identity. When customers see your logo or packaging, it should evoke immediate recognition, connecting them to the values and story you've crafted for your brand.

9

Selling Your Honey Products

I n this chapter, we explore marketing strategies tailored specifically for honey products. Let's explore practical and effective methods for presenting your honey offerings to consumers. Strategies range from leveraging social media to forming partnerships with local businesses, all with the primary goal of establishing meaningful connections with customers. Highlighting how great and flexible honey is, seeking to capture the attention of a diverse audience.

Strategies such as active participation in farmers' markets, organizing tasting events, and curating informative online content foster trust and loyalty among consumers. With a steadfast commitment to authenticity and community engagement, these marketing endeavors are designed to cultivate enduring relationships and stimulate sales within a competitive market environment.

Farmers' Markets

Before you start selling your honey at farmers' markets, it's essential to do some research. Explore nearby local markets, considering factors such as their location, size, and typical product offerings. Visit these markets to see how things work, understand the people who come, and check out what others sell.

Compliance and Permits

Learn about the rules and permissions to sell honey at local markets. Contact your area's health department and other authorities to ensure you follow all the rules. This might mean getting licenses, following health and safety rules, and ensuring correct labels.

Stall Set-Up and Display

Set up a welcoming stand that shows off what makes your honey unique. Think about how it looks so it's pretty and shows off your brand. Make a neat, friendly display that lets customers see your honey products easily. Put up signs that point out important things, like the types of honey you have, what's in them, and why they're special.

Pricing and Packaging

Set competitive and profitable prices for your honey creations by researching similar products. Explore various sizes or packaging options to accommodate different customer preferences. Ensure clear labeling with prices and include pertinent information, such as using organic or locally sourced ingredients.

Building a Loyal Local Customer Base

Build meaningful connections with your customers by engaging in conversations and providing insights into your unique honey creations. Share your passion for the distinct qualities of your products. Creating a friendly and approachable atmosphere enhances the customer experience and fosters loyalty.

Loyalty Programs

Implement loyalty programs to reward repeat customers. This could involve offering discounts, free samples, or exclusive access to new products. Loyalty programs encourage customer retention and serve as a marketing tool, as satisfied customers are likely to spread the word.

Community Engagement

Get involved in your local community to build trust and strengthen your brand. Go to local events, support community projects, and team up with nearby businesses. Doing these things makes more people know about your brand and shows that you care about and contribute to the community.

Host a Honey Tasting Event

Hosting a honey-tasting event combines fun, education, and a great way to market your honey and honey products. Attendees indulge in diverse honey flavors, expanding their palate. Experts can share insights on beekeeping, pollination, and environmental impact, fostering awareness.

The event generates positive buzz, creating memorable experiences that translate into brand loyalty and word-of-mouth promotion, amplifying marketing efforts.

Encourage customer reviews and testimonials. Positive experiences shared by real customers build trust and authenticity around your brand.

You can invite local influencers to your tasting at no cost. Influencers may benefit by producing fun content for their page as well.

The Art of Honey Tasting/Host an Event

Tasting honey is like going on a flavor adventure! It is about trying different types, and you use all your senses to enjoy the different tastes, smells, and textures. To master the art of honey tasting, consider the following steps:

Visual

Start by looking at the color and clarity of the honey. Various flowers give honey different colors, from light gold to deep amber. The transparency can also change, showing you how thick the honey is.

Aroma

Gently swirl the honey in the jar to release its aroma. Inhale deeply and identify the fragrance notes. Floral varieties might carry the scents of lavender or jasmine, while others may hint at fruity or herbal undertones.

Tasting Technique

Try a little spoonful of honey and let it coat your palate. Take your time, and notice the changing flavors. First, you might taste sweetness, then discover hints of citrus, woodiness, or spice.

Texture

Pay attention to the texture as the honey coats your mouth. Some honey is smooth and creamy, while others may crystallize, offering a delightful crunch. The mouthfeel can vary from silky to thick and gooey, adding another layer to the tasting experience.

Examples of Honey Varieties

Acacia Honey - Delicate and light, with a pale color and floral notes. It is ideal for those new to honey tasting.

Manuka Honey - Hails from New Zealand is known for its robust flavor profile with earthy and medicinal notes. It is often prized for its potential health benefits.

Orange Blossom Honey - Citrusy and fragrant, with a golden color. Perfect for adding a sweet and aromatic touch to various dishes.

Pairing Honey with Food and Drinks

The versatility of honey can be a delightful complement to many dishes and beverages. Here's a guide to pairing honey with various foods and drinks:

Cheese and Honey Pairing - Honey pairs exceptionally well with various cheeses, creating a harmony of sweet and savory flavors. Try drizzling honey over a soft, creamy Brie or pairing it with a sharp blue cheese.

Tea and Honey Pairing - Experiment with different honey varieties in your tea. For black tea, a robust honey-like chestnut complements the bold flavors, while lighter teas like green or white pair well with the delicacy of acacia or clover honey.

Honey and Nut Combinations - Spread honey over toast with a generous almond or peanut butter layer for a delicious and nutritious breakfast. The natural sweetness of honey enhances the nutty flavors.

Fruit and Honey Pairing - Drizzle honey over fresh fruit salads or use it as a glaze for roasted fruits. The sweetness of honey intensifies the natural sugars in the fruit, creating a harmonious blend of flavors.

Meat and Honey Pairing - Use honey as a glaze for grilled or roasted meats. The caramelization adds depth, and the sweetness balances the savory notes. Honey can enhance the flavors of dishes like honey-glazed ham or honey-soy chicken.

Pairings with Honey Flavors

Blue Cheese and Tupelo Honey - The bold and tangy notes of blue cheese are beautifully complemented by the mellow sweetness of Tupelo honey, creating a harmonious balance on the palate.

Chamomile Tea with Lavender Honey - The soothing qualities of chamomile tea are accentuated by the aromatic lavender honey, creating a calming and fragrant beverage.

Grilled Peaches with Wildflower Honey - The natural sweetness of grilled peaches is elevated with a drizzle of wildflower honey, creating a simple yet decadent dessert.

Monofloral Honey is produced by bees that primarily collect nectar from a single type of flower, resulting in a distinctive aroma and flavor profile unique to that floral source. Examples include lavender honey or orange blossom honey. On the other hand, *Polyfloral Honey*, also known as wildflower honey, is derived from various flowers, offering a more diverse and blended taste. It captures the essence of the surrounding flora, providing a well-rounded and nuanced flavor experience. Each option, monofloral and polyfloral, offers a different taste adventure for honey enthusiasts.

The Honey Tasting Event

Throwing a honey-tasting event is a fun way for both honey lovers and newbies to dive into the world of honey. Whether it's a cozy get-together or a more prominent public event, here are some examples of honey-tasting event activities to make your honey-tasting adventure a success:

Educational Sessions

Begin the event with a brief educational session on honey tasting. Share some basics about the different kinds of honey and what bees do, and explore how the honey's location, or "terroir," affects the taste.

"Meet the Beekeeper"

Collaborate with local beekeepers to add a personal touch to the event. Inviting them to share insights into beekeeping practices and honey production adds depth to the educational component. This personal connection adds authenticity to the event.

Tasting Stations

Offer a diverse selection of honey varieties, including monofloral and polyfloral options, allowing participants to explore the range of flavors and aromas present in different kinds of honey.

Set up tasting stations with various small jars of honey, accompanied by tasting spoons and palate cleansers such as water and neutral crackers. Label each honey variety to guide participants through the tasting process.

DIY Honey Pairing Station and Demonstration

Set up a station with various foods, drinks, and honey varieties. Include live demonstrations on pairing honey with foods and beverages. Get everyone involved by letting them taste these combinations, showing how honey can be used in different types of cooking. Allow participants to experiment with creating their unique pairings.

Blind Tasting Challenge

Blindfold participants to taste different honey varieties and have them try to identify the floral sources. It is a fun and interactive way to test their palate.

Promote Your Products and Events

For successful marketing at farmers' markets, use social media, team up with other sellers, send emails, and match promotions with seasons and holidays. It's not just about having great honey; it's also about the relationships you create and the stories you share.

Use social media to excite people about your presence at farmers' markets. Share cool pictures, show what's happening behind the scenes, and give updates about your products. Invite your followers to come to your stand by offering special deals or discounts just for them.

Collaborations and Cross-Promotions

Explore collaborations with other vendors at the farmers' market. Cross-promotions can introduce your honey creations to a broader audience. For instance, collaborate with a local bakery to create honey-infused pastries or collaborate with a fruit vendor for joint promotions.

Collecting Customer Feedback

Ask your customers for feedback. Find out what they like and expect. This information helps make your products better and give customers what they want. Being open to feedback shows that you're always trying to improve things, tailoring your offerings to meet customer needs.

Seasonal and Holiday Promotions

Plan your marketing strategy with the seasons and holidays in mind. Make unique honey products for different times of the year or put together themed gift sets for holidays. Highlight how unique and versatile your honey is, making it a perfect gift for special occasions.

Selling your honey at farmers' markets and local outlets brings opportunities and challenges. You'll need good planning, follow the rules, and make your products look appealing to navigate these. To build loyal customers locally, focus on personal connections, loyalty programs, community involvement, and getting feedback regularly.

Remember, success is an ongoing process. Listen to what customers say, understand local market trends, and be ready to adjust your plans. With careful planning, community involvement, and smart marketing, your honey can do well in local sales and be a part of the lively local community.

Savoring the World of Honey

Tasting and pairing honey is like taking a delicious trip into the fantastic world of this golden treat. Whether you love trying different kinds or a beekeeper sharing your honey, tasting honey turns it from a sweet treat into a whole adventure for your senses. Having honey-tasting events makes it even more fun because everyone can enjoy and discover this timeless culinary treasure together. So, as you dive into the world of honey, enjoy every drop, savor its different flavors, and have fun trying all the ways you can pair honey with different foods.

10

Online Sales & Social Media

I f the idea of selling your products online has crossed your mind, this chapter will guide you through the initial steps. While I'm not an expert website builder, there are platforms like Fiverr or Upwork where you can find professionals to create a fantastic website for your honey business. It's worth noting that I don't receive any compensation for recommending these companies—it's just a helpful suggestion to kick start your honey hustle.

Choosing the Right E-commerce Platform to Set up an Online Store

Select a reliable e-commerce platform that aligns with your business needs. Popular options include Shopify, WooCommerce, and BigCommerce. Consider factors like ease of use, customization options, and transaction fees. Do your research to find the best fit for your business.

Designing Your Online Store

Create a professional and user-friendly website that showcases your honey-inspired products and brand story. Ensure the website looks and feels like you, using the same colors, fonts, and images that promote your brand. Place your mission statement where everyone can see it so they get why your creations are fantastic.

Simplify the process for customers to explore your site, from shopping to completing their purchase. Keep in mind that not all users are proficient in using computers.

Product Listings and Descriptions

Create detailed product listings that highlight the unique qualities of your honey creations. Include information about the floral source, flavor profile, and unique features. Engaging product descriptions helps customers make informed decisions. Ask a friend to sample your products and read your descriptions. Choose someone who will give you their best critique.

Secure Payment Gateways

Add safe and trustworthy payment methods for easy transactions. Provide various payment choices like credit cards, digital wallets, and other popular options to suit customer preferences.

Implementing Search Engine Optimization (SEO) Strategies

Improve your online store's visibility using relevant keywords in product titles, descriptions, and meta tags. Keep your website content up-to-date, and think about starting a blog to share valuable information about honey and beekeeping.

Important E-commerce Best Practices

User-Friendly Navigation

Make sure visitors can easily navigate your site. Arrange products into categories and use filters to simplify searching. Use clear calls-to-action for actions like "Add to Cart" and "Checkout."

Mobile Optimization

Since more people are shopping on mobile devices, ensure your online store works well on them. Test the user experience on smartphones and tablets to ensure everything runs smoothly. Don't lose a sale to a poor mobile device experience.

Customer Reviews

Show customer reviews and testimonials to build trust. Positive feedback from happy customers helps convince new shoppers to buy. Set up a review system and ask customers to share their experiences. Think about how many times you check a review when purchasing online. Customer Reviews are vital!

Promotions and Discounts

Use promotions and discounts strategically to attract and keep customers. Provide special deals for first-time customers, create bundle discounts, or establish loyalty programs for repeat buyers. Clearly explain the terms of promotions on your website. There is nothing more gratifying than a repeat customer!

Email Marketing Campaigns

Create a list of customers who opt-in to receive updates and promotions via email. Use email marketing campaigns to introduce new products, share informative content about honey, and offer exclusive deals. Personalized email communication helps strengthen the relationship with your customer base.

Shipping and Online Customer Service

Efficient Order Fulfillment

Make your order fulfillment process smooth for on-time and accurate deliveries. Invest in trustworthy shipping partners and use shipping management tools to track orders. Give customers tracking information to keep them updated on their shipments.

State Shipping Costs

State shipping costs during checkout. Offering free shipping for orders over a certain amount can encourage customers to add more items to their cart. Alternatively, use accurate shipping calculators for transparency. Don't slam a potential buyer with unreasonable shipping costs at the end of a great shopping experience.

Online Customer Service

Set up a quick and helpful online customer service system. Provide various ways for customers to reach out, such as email, chat, and social media. Respond promptly to their questions and address issues with a customer-focused approach.

Returns and Refunds Policies

Clearly state your return and refund policies to manage customer expectations. A straightforward and transparent process for handling returns or refunds contributes to a positive customer experience, even if there's an issue.

Personalized Packaging

Add personal touches to your packaging, like handwritten thank-you notes, recipe cards, or small samples of other honey varieties. Thoughtful packaging improves the unboxing experience and leaves a lasting impression.

When you sell honey products online, you can connect with more customers. Set up a fantastic online store, follow selling tips, and provide excellent customer service to help your honey business grow. Pay attention to customer preferences and honey trends. Keep your online store interesting by adding new products and engaging with customers on social media and through emails (keep an organized customer email list). Following the best online selling practices can make your honey business successful in the busy world of online sales.

Social Media

Use social media to connect with your audience. Share good-looking content that shows your brand – like behind-the-scenes of making honey, customer stories, or posts about honey benefits. Regular posting and talking with your audience help people get to know and trust your brand.

Content Marketing

Create a content plan that reflects your brand and resonates with your target audience. Write blogs or make videos about honey, Eco-friendliness, and health. Aim to be seen as an authority in your field, demonstrating that your brand is authentic. Consider collaborating with influencers or experts who share your interests. Their endorsement can increase your visibility and build trust with a broader audience.

Hire a Content Creator

Hiring a content creator offers invaluable benefits for enhancing your brand's online presence. They specialize in crafting tailored, engaging content across various platforms, boosting visibility and audience engagement. With their expertise, you save time and resources while ensuring consistent, high-quality content that fosters brand loyalty and drives growth.

Not sure what a content creator does? Here is a great example:
malloryann.my.canva.site/smm

Visual Storytelling

Enhance the appeal of your stories by incorporating captivating visuals such as pictures, videos, and cool graphics. Craft and share your brand story visually on platforms like Instagram, Pinterest, and YouTube, offering excellent opportunities to display attractive visuals and connect with your customers. Utilize a mix of captivating imagery and engaging videos to make your brand presence memorable and foster a deeper connection with customers.

Interactive Content

Create fun quizzes, polls, and surveys to engage customers in your brand story. When they join in, it makes them feel connected and invested in what's happening with your brand.

Social Media Narratives

Leverage social media as a platform for storytelling to promote honey sales. Share concise stories, behind-the-scenes insights, and success stories from satisfied customers on platforms like Facebook, Twitter, and LinkedIn. These channels provide opportunities for immediate interaction and feedback from your audience.

Shaping Your Brand's Image Over Time

Think of your brand like a living thing. As your business grows, your brand identity should grow with it. Take some time now and then to check if your brand values still match how you run your business. See if your brand story needs a minor update based on new things that have happened.

Also, look at your logo and packaging design from time to time. Does it still connect with the people you're trying to reach, or is it time for a change? Trends shift, and your brand should stay in the loop.

Keep an ear out for what customers say and what's hot in the market. This information can help you tweak your marketing plan or inspire new products. It's like giving your brand a checkup to keep it healthy and up-to-date.

Making your honey products stand out involves getting what matters to you, telling a great story, and thinking about how things look. Once you figure this out, ensure it shows everywhere you talk about your products so people always remember you. As your brand grows, keep tweaking things to ensure it still fits what you're all about and what your customers love. With a well-thought-out brand, your honey creations can make a lasting impression on people's hearts and taste buds worldwide.

11

Advertising & Networking Tips

In today's digital era, advertising your products has never been easier. From free options to paid ones, the opportunities are vast. Here are some simple ways to start promoting your products today, using just your smartphone to snap photos.

Examples of Online Advertising:

Instagram Carousel Ads

Create carousel ads displaying different honey varieties or perhaps gift sets on Instagram. Each slide can focus on flavors, pairings, or customer reviews, making the ad more engaging and informative.

Google Shopping Campaigns

Set up Google Shopping campaigns for your artisanal honey products. Use good images, clear descriptions, and competitive prices. Google

Shopping ads appear prominently in search results, helping more people find and buy your products.

Pinterest Ads

Advertising on Pinterest can effectively reach a highly engaged audience, particularly if your target demographic aligns with Pinterest's user base, which tends to skew toward women and people interested in lifestyle, fashion, home decor, DIY projects, food, and similar topics.

Active Social Media Presence

Stay active on social media. Respond quickly to comments, messages, and mentions. Engage people by asking questions, running polls, and seeking their opinions. Showing the personal side of your brand creates a sense of community. Please don't engage in negativity. There will always be someone willing to burst your bubble. If it is something you feel can be fixed, by all means, fix it! If you think it is trash talk…keep scrolling! Do not engage.

Educational Content

Share helpful content about honey, beekeeping, and the artisanal process. Use blogs, infographics, or video tutorials to give valuable info to your audience. Make your brand a trusted source in the honey world, building trust and credibility.

User-Generated Content (UGC) Campaigns

Start campaigns for user-generated content (UGC) to get your audience involved. Ask customers to share photos, recipes, or stories with your honey products. Highlight and feature this content on social media to build a sense of community and appreciation.

Examples of Audience Engagement:

Recipe Challenge on Twitter

Start a recipe challenge on Twitter. Ask followers to share their favorite recipes using your honey. Use a specific hashtag for the challenge and reward participants with mentions, discounts, or a chance to collaborate on a new product.

Monthly Educational Series on Instagram

Begin a monthly educational series on Instagram about honey, bees, and sustainability. Use a mix of carousel posts, IGTV videos, and live sessions to share valuable insights. Invite questions and engagement from your audience during the series.

Nurturing Your Online Presence for Artisanal Honey Success

A robust online presence will be vital for your artisanal honey business in the digital age. Use social media, targeted online ads, and engage with your audience. Stay updated on audience preferences, follow trends, and uphold authenticity. Combining these strategies allows you to expand your reach and build a loyal online community that appreciates your unique honey creations.

Networking

Industry Insights and Knowledge Sharing

Networking in the honey business goes beyond making connections; it's a valuable opportunity to gain insights and share knowledge. Engaging with fellow beekeepers, honey producers, and industry experts lets you stay updated on the latest trends, innovations, and challenges in the apiculture and honey market.

Access to Resources and Support

Building a network provides valuable resources and support systems. Whether you need advice on hive management, sourcing high-quality jars, or navigating regulatory requirements, a well-established network can offer guidance and assistance. Establishing relationships within the industry fosters a sense of collaboration and shared success.

Participating in Industry Events

Attend beekeeping conferences, agricultural fairs, and food expos to connect with fellow artisans in the honey industry. These events provide a platform for face-to-face interactions, allowing you to exchange ideas, discuss best practices, and establish relationships with like-minded individuals passionate about honey and beekeeping.

Joining Beekeeping Associations and Groups

Become an active member of beekeeping associations, both local and national. Participating in these groups provides opportunities to build relationships with fellow artisans. Share your experiences, learn from others, and contribute to the collective knowledge of the beekeeping community. Online forums and social media groups also offer virtual spaces for networking.

Collaborative Hive Projects

Collaborate with fellow artisans on hive projects that benefit both parties. This could involve sharing apiaries, jointly organizing honey extraction events, or collaborating on sustainable beekeeping initiatives. By working together, you can pool resources, share costs, and create a supportive community of beekeepers.

Collaborative Marketing Strategies

Cross-promotions with Artisanal Products

Collaborate with fellow artisans on cross-promotional initiatives, such as local cheese makers, bakers, or craft brewers. Bundle your honey products with theirs for special promotions or create unique pairings that appeal to a broader audience. This expands your reach and introduces your honey to customers with diverse interests.

Joint Marketing Campaigns

Launch joint marketing campaigns with fellow artisans to amplify your collective impact, such as co-hosting events, creating shared content on social media, or even collaborating on a regional marketing campaign that promotes local artisanal products. Leveraging each other's audiences enhances the visibility of all participating businesses.

Partnerships with Retailers and Restaurants

Form partnerships with local retailers and restaurants that align with your honey business's artisanal and sustainable ethos. Work together on exclusive product launches, in-store promotions, or honey-themed menu items. These partnerships create a win-win scenario, driving foot traffic for the retailers and introducing your honey to a broader audience.

Educational Workshops and Tastings

Organize joint educational workshops or honey tastings with fellow artisans. This collaborative approach provides valuable content for your audience and showcases the diversity of artisanal products available. Could you consider partnering with local chefs or nutritionists to enhance the educational aspect of these events?

Examples of Collaborative Marketing Success:

Local Farmers' Market Collaboration
Partner with other local crafters at the farmers' market to have a more significant presence. Plan how your booths look, do promotions together, and show how well your honey goes with other local goodies. Working together like this can bring in more people and make the market lively and fun.

Seasonal Collaboration with a Bakery
Work together with a nearby bakery for a special seasonal promotion. Make a unique pastry or dessert with your honey and their delicious

baked treats. Tell people about this partnership on social media and through your customer networks to get as many interested as possible.

Nurturing Connections for Sweet Success

Networking and building relationships are essential for your honey business to do well. Embrace the opportunities to connect with fellow artisans, beekeepers, and people in the industry. Through collaborative marketing strategies and shared endeavors, you not only strengthen your brand but also contribute to the growth and vibrancy of the artisanal honey community.

As you engage in networking activities and build relationships, remember that authenticity and mutual support are essential. Whether sharing insights with a fellow beekeeper or co-hosting an event with a local artisan, the connections you forge contribute to a thriving ecosystem that benefits everyone involved. Nurturing these relationships is an investment in the longevity and sweetness of your honey business.

12

Conclusion - The Sweet Road to Success

Share the Sweetness

As you continue on the sweet road ahead, your journey into the world of honey has been personal, and now it's time to share the sweetness with others. Whether through educating, reaching out to the community, or starting your honey-centric business, the road ahead is filled with opportunities to spread the joy of honey. Your knowledge is a beacon, and the world awaits your contribution to understanding and appreciating nature's gift—this liquid gold.

Bee a Changemaker

The sweet road ahead is about positively impacting the world. Consider becoming an advocate for bee conservation, supporting local beekeepers, or collaborating with organizations that champion sustainable practices. Your journey has equipped you with knowledge and passion—use them to become a changemaker in the larger ecological landscape.

Never Stop Exploring

Throughout our journey, we've immersed ourselves in the captivating history of honey, savored its delightful flavors in countless recipes, and marveled at the diverse array of honey-based products. From age-old customs to contemporary culinary delights, honey has become integral to our cultural and gastronomic tapestry. As you step into your honey-filled hustle, I encourage you to embrace creative marketing approaches, whether it's teaming up with local artisans or organizing honey-tasting gatherings, to spread your enthusiasm for this golden elixir. May the wisdom gained enrich your appreciation for honey and ignite innovative strategies that propel your endeavors toward triumph and fulfillment.

As we wrap up our journey through the captivating world of honey, let it inspire further exploration. Stay curious, for the world of honey is brimming with hidden treasures waiting to be uncovered.

If you found this book helpful, I'd be most appreciative if you left a favorable review for the book on Amazon.

13

References

Nemours Childrens Health. (2023, February). Why Should Babies Not Have Honey? kidshealth.org. Retrieved February 4, 2024, from https://kidshealth.org/en/parents/honey-botulism.prt-en.html

The story of Demeter and Persephone. (n.d.-b). The Fitzwilliam Museum. Retrieved February 4, 2024, from https://fitzmuseum.cam.ac.uk/learn-with-us/the-story-of-demeter-and-persephone

The Book of Love Quotes by Rumi (Jalal Ad-Din Muhammad Ar-Rumi). (n.d.). goodreads.com. Retrieved February 4, 2024, from https://www.goodreads.com/work/quotes/65340-rumi-the-book-of-love-poems-of-ecstasy-and-longing

Geronimus, D. (2022, October 27). The discovery of Honey by Bacchus. Wikipedia. Retrieved February 4, 2024, from https://en.wikipedia.org/wiki/The_Discovery_of_Honey_by_Bacchus

Hive, F. (2023, September 19). How do bees make honey? Flow Hive

US. Retrieved February 4, 2024, from https://www.honeyflow.com/bl ogs/beekeeping-basics/how-do-bees-make-honey

Be Smart. (2016b, March 28). How do bees make honey? [Video]. YouTube. Retrieved February 4, 2024, from https://www.youtube.com /watch?v=nZlEjDLJCmg

DIY Elderberry Honey Lollipops: a natural sore throat remedy made with just 2 ingredients. (2023, November 9). Elderberry Queen. Retrieved February 4, 2024, from https://www.elderberryqueen.ne t/blogs/recipes/elderberry-honey-lollipops

Cover: Photo by ROMAN ODINTSOV: https://www.pexels.com/phot o/honey-on-plate-and-spoon-6422025/